A0212971
P9-DOA-483

SENECA
WITHDRAWN
COLLEGE LIBRARY

Wild Animals by Brian Wildsmith

A herd of reindeer

For Simon

A crash of rhinoceroses

Wild Animals by Brian Wildsmith

London OXFORD UNIVERSITY PRESS

A sloth of bears

A nursery of racoons

A herd of hippopotami

An ambush
of tigers

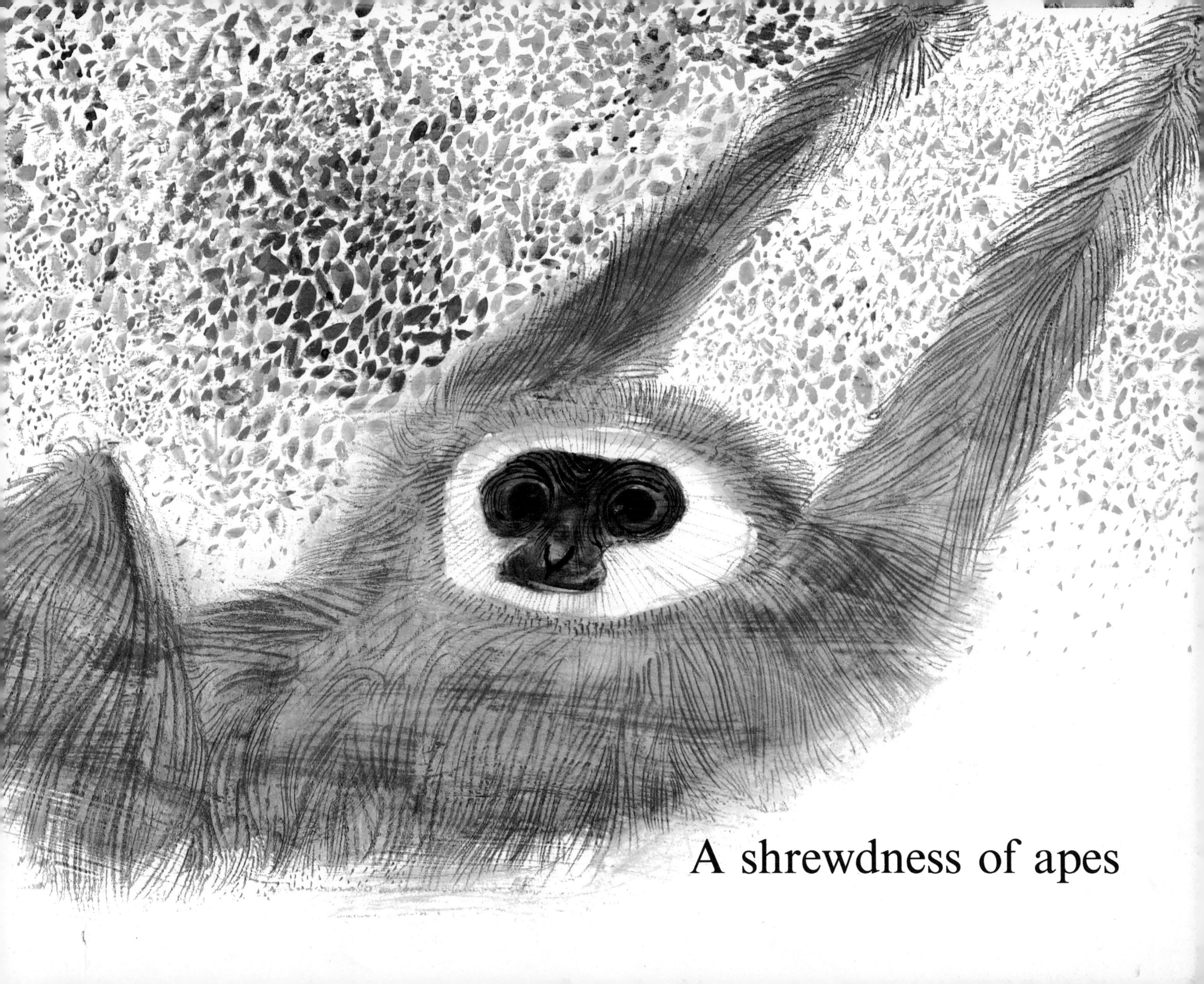

A shrewdness of apes

A pride of lions

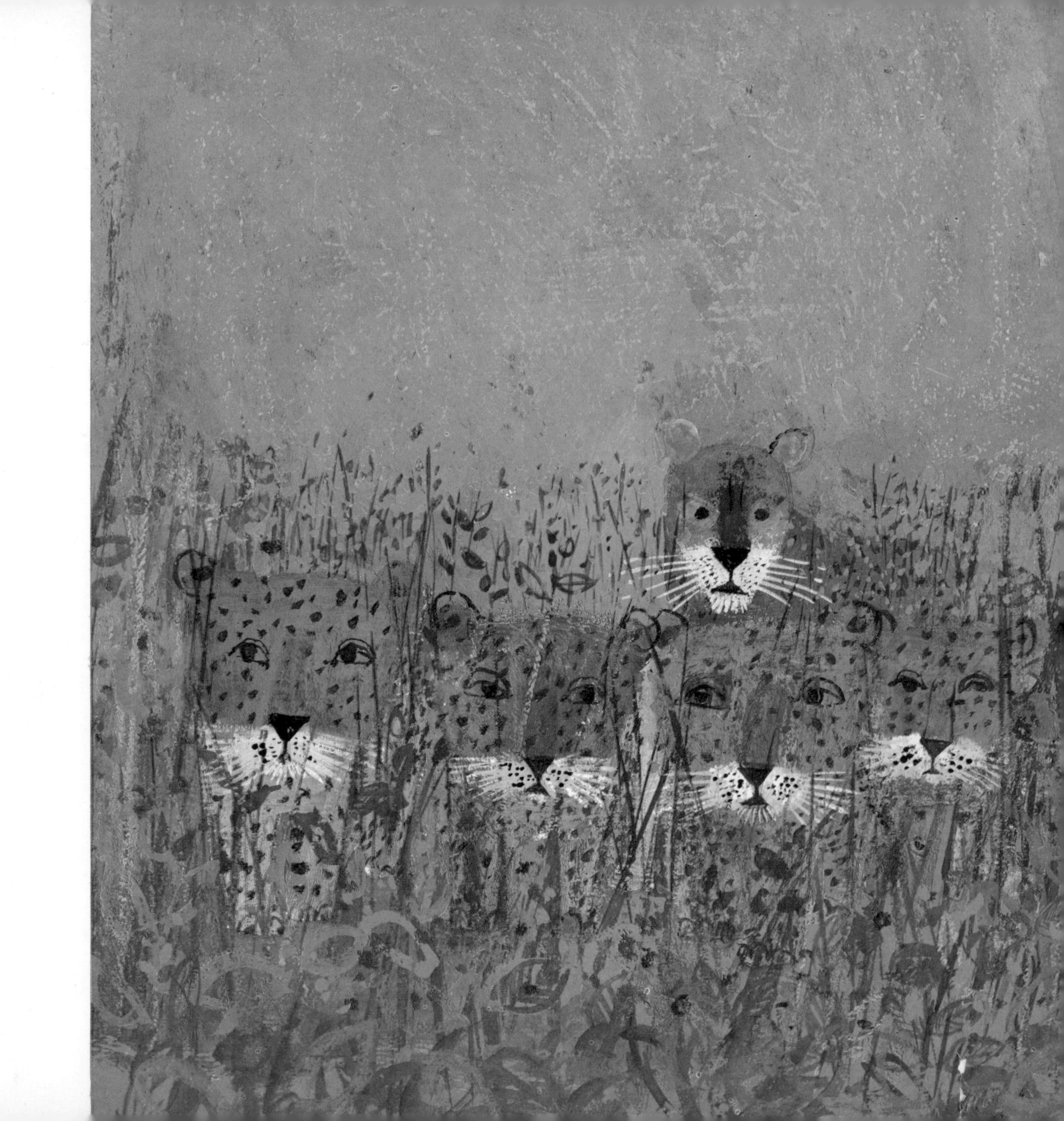

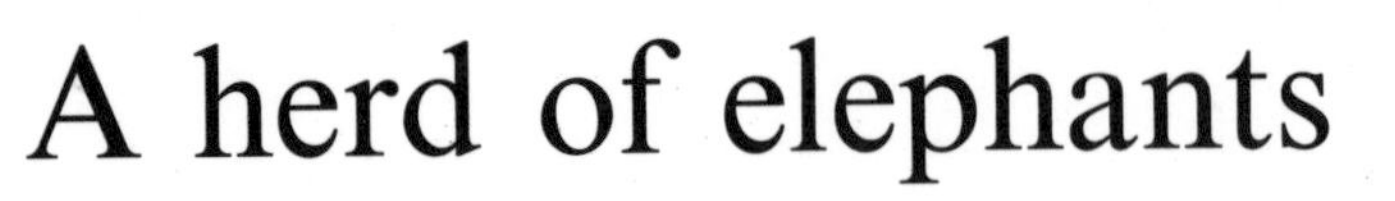

A herd of elephants

A lepe of leopards

A corps of giraffes

A troop of kangaroos

A skulk of foxes

A family of otters

A cete of badgers

An array
of hedgehogs

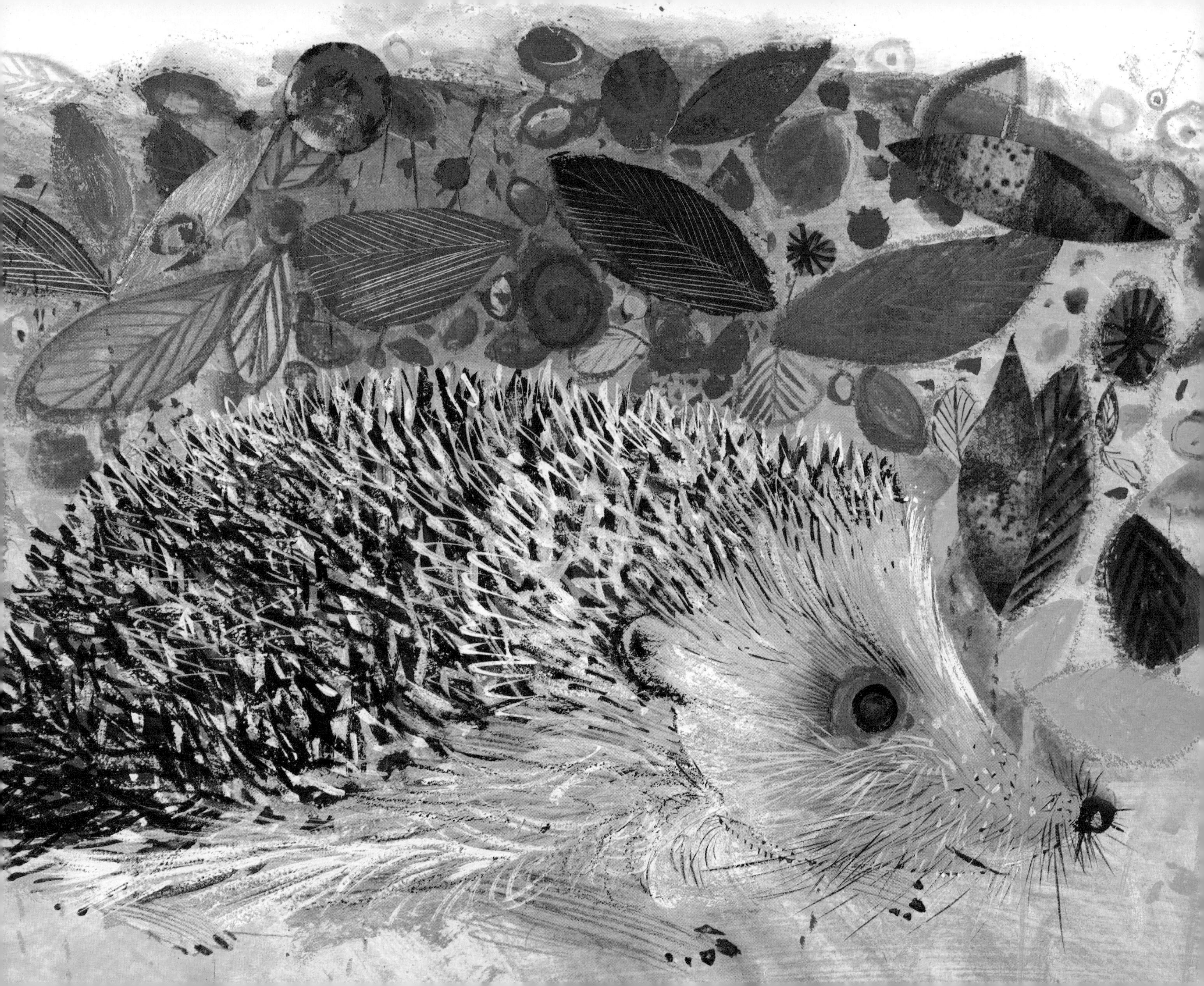

Oxford University Press, Ely House, London W.1 GLASGOW NEW YORK TORONTO MELBOURNE
WELLINGTON CAPE TOWN SALISBURY IBADAN NAIROBI DAR ES SALAAM LUSAKA ADDIS ABABA BOMBAY CALCUTTA
MADRAS KARACHI LAHORE DACCA KUALA LUMPUR SINGAPORE HONG KONG TOKYO

 FIRST PUBLISHED 1967. REPRINTED 1968, 1970, 1971

PRINTED IN AUSTRIA

SENECA
WITHDRAWN
LEGE LIBRA